FRONTISPIECE

Birkenhead Iron Works (Laird's) in the 1860's.
Illustration: Williamson Art Gallery, Birkenhead.

FRONT COVER

A Merchantman burns while a confederate ship slips away into the night.
Artist's impression by Eric Monks.

BACK COVER

The Confederate Sloop-of-War "290," or Alabama, leaving the Merchant-ship Tonowanda.
Illustration: London Illus. News.

Ghost Ships of the Mersey

A brief history of Confederate cruisers with Mersey connections

by
K.J. Williams

Published by:

Countyvise Limited,
1 & 3 Grove Road, Rock Ferry, Birkenhead,
Merseyside. L42 3XS.

ISBN 0 907768 10 5

All royalties from the sale of this book
are vested in The Merseyside Confederate Navy History Society

*Printed in England by: BIRKENHEAD PRESS LTD.,
1 & 3 Grove Road, Rock Ferry, Birkenhead, Merseyside. L42 3XS.*

FOREWORD

I hope with the publication of this booklet that a famous part of Merseyside history will be explained. The vessels involved are two Confederate naval cruisers built on the Mersey and two that were later to surrender to the authorities here. One of the vessels the Alabama is arguably the most famous ship ever to sail from our local shores. The importance of these four cruisers to the Confederacy was immense, leading to the situation after the American Civil War, that the United States demanded millions of dollars compensation for the damage caused to their merchant fleet by the presence of these vessels on the high seas. Besides the Monitor-Merrimac ironclad dual this was the second most important naval event to arise from the civil war. For naval ships to prey on its enemy's merchant fleet brought out a new concept in marine warfare to be copied by Germany in later wars.

THE CAUSES OF THE AMERICAN CIVIL WAR

The election of Abraham Lincoln as President of the United States in 1860 was the culminating event that led to the break up of the Union. The Southern States were not prepared to accept a Republican Government dedicated to the abolition of slavery.

On December 20th, 1860, South Carolina seceded from the Union, followed by the States of Alabama, Florida, Mississippi, Georgia, Louisiana, and Texas. Many hoped that secession would be a peaceful exercise but problems arose almost immediately. There were many Federal Garrisons located in and around the harbours of various Southern ports, and at Fort Sumter in Charleston Harbour the occupants refused to withdraw. On April 12th, 1861, the Southern batteries opened fire. For thirty-four hours the bombardment lasted before Major Roberts Anderson surrendered. President Lincoln issued a call for 75,000 troops to "suppress the rebellion".

This was interpreted by the Southern States of Virginia, North Carolina, Tennessee and Arkansas as a declaration of war. They in turn seceded and formed a Confederacy with the other dissenting States.

The outbreak of hostilities found the Southern States in the worst position for ensuing hostilities. The North had a ten to one advantage in manufacturing, two to one in manpower and thirty to one in arms production. Although the Union at the start of the war had only forty five ships available, this would soon be increased substantially because of their capacity to build new ships. The South because of its lack of resources was forced to turn to Europe. This situation brought James Dunwoody Bulloch to Liverpool as a ship purchasing agent for the Confederacy.

JAMES DUNWOODY BULLOCH

James Dunwoody Bulloch a native of Georgia, had a long naval career behind him at the outbreak of hostilities in the Civil War. He had served in the U.S. Navy during the Mexican War as a Lieutenant. Later when congress stated that mail steamers should be commanded by Naval Officers, Bulloch was put in command of the Black Warrior sailing between New York and the Gulf ports. Dissapointed with promotion in the U.S. Navy Bulloch resigned to take up a captaincy under the firm which owned the mail steamers. In command of the Bienville in 1861 and realising war was imminent he sailed his ship back to its owners in New York. (Being well able to surrender it to the Confederacy, but Bulloch's high sense of business honour forbade this.) After handing in his resignation to an understanding company director, he made his way to the Southern States.

James Dunwoody Bulloch reported for duty at the Confederate Navy Department at Montgomery, Alabama on May 8th, 1861. On orders of Stephen R. Mallory, Secretary of the Navy, he proceeded to England via Canada arriving in Liverpool on June 4th. His orders from Mallory were to buy, or have constructed, six steam vessels suitable for use as commerce destroyers against the Union, to be delivered, unarmed under the British flag at any Southern port. In addition, he was to buy and run arms for the Cruisers.

After being in touch with Southern Diplomatic Commissioners as well as Fraser Trenholm & Co (Foreign Bankers for the Confederacy), Bulloch's next stop was to find a good lawyer. One F.S. Hull of Liverpool, "prudent, cautious and conscientious", proved to be just the man to point out the weaknesses of the Queen's Neutrality Proclamation[1] and the Foreign Enlistment Act.[2]

With the legal difficulties solved, Bulloch began scanning the registry lists of shipping. Finding nothing suitable, he signed a contract with Fawcett & Preston, Engineers, and W.C. Miller & Son to build a steam sloop (see C.S.S. Florida). She was delivered in December, 1861.

Left: Stephen R. Mallory. Right: James D. Bulloch.
Photos: U.S. Navy Photo Department Washington D.C.

The second contract was signed in late July, 1861 with Laird Brothers and work began on the 290 (it was Laird's 290th vessel). In the meantime, Bulloch acquired a thirteen-knot screw-steamer, the Fingal, and he sailed with it loaded with arms and ammunition through the Union Blockade and landed at Savannah, Georgia, returning to Liverpool on 10th March 1862. As the arrangements for the 290 (or Enrica — Bulloch's fictitious name for the ship) neared completion, Bulloch realised that he would have to work fast. He was well informed of the activities of U.S. Minister to Great Britain Charles Francis Adams, and of the affidavits being collected by this industrious New Englander and his consular colleagues.

Above Left: Grave of James D. Bulloch, Toxteth Cemetery, Liverpool.
Above Right and Below Left: Inscriptions on Grave.
Below Right: Offices of Fraser Trenholm and James D. Bulloch, 10 Rumford Place, Liverpool.

On 29th, July the 290 went to sea, supposedly on a trial trip with various dignatories aboard. A short distance from shore, however, the passengers were transferred to a tug and returned to port while the ship sailed down the coast to Anglesey, then to the north coast of Ireland, where the pilot and Bulloch were landed. She arrived at the Island of Terceira in the Azores in mid-August to take on armaments and ammunition, from the supply ship, Agrippina.

Bulloch was involved in more ship-buying exercises until the end of the Civil War, including the Laird's Rams[3] (Nos 294 & 295) which were impounded by the Government and eventually sold to the Royal Navy. Bulloch stayed in Liverpool after the war and involved himself in many business activities until his death in early January, 1901. He is buried in Smithdown Road Cemetery, Toxteth.

[1] On May 13th 1861 the Queen announced recognition of Confederate belligerency. The Proclamation was made in reaction to the outbreak of hostilities in America.

[2] Union and Confederate vessels could use port facilities only for repairs they could not increase their crews or armament or take on contraband etc.

[3] Lairds Rams took their name from the Iron-Piercer of great strength which protruded six to seven feet beyond the prow. When the vessel was in motion the spur remained three to four feet below the water line thus enabling it to strike an opponent below the water line.

Illustration: London Illus. News.

Laird's Ram later named H.M.S. Scorpion.

C.S.S. FLORIDA

As already mentioned, James Dunwoody Bulloch, the Confederate Agent, on his arrival in Liverpool lost no time in contacting William C. Miller & Son (Shipbuilders) and Fawcett & Preston (Engineers) and agreements were signed for a vessel to be built. Fawcetts would handle the financial details, and design and construct the engines. William C. Miller would supply the hull, masts and rigging. By the beginning of July 1861 work had started. The ship was to be known to her builders as the Oreto, an Italian name chosen by Bulloch to put the suspicious off the scent.

The activities of Bulloch had not gone unnoticed. The U.S. Consul in Liverpool, Thomas H. Dudley, with offices situated in Tower Buildings, South Water Street, reported to his superior, the U.S. Ambassador in London, Charles Adams, "there is much secrecy about the Oreto but my impressions are strong that she is intended for the Southern Confederacy". He later reported that "no pains or expense have been spared in her construction and when fully armed she will be a formidable and dangerous craft".

Disturbed by his Consul's reports, Adams complained to the Foreign Office that the building of the Oreto was a violation of Britain's declaration of neutrality. The Foreign Office disagreed, for Bulloch had been most careful to keep strictly within the law, depositing nothing aboard the Oreto that could be described as equipment of war. On the 22nd March, 1862, the Oreto sailed from Liverpool, ostensibly for Palermo but actually for Nassau in the Bahamas, pretending to be a merchant vessel. Guns, ammunition and stores followed in a British cargo ship. By August she had been commissioned into the Confederate Navy and renamed Florida, made ready for action, and soon sailed from Nassau under Captain J.N. Maffitt.

CONFEDERATE CRUISER *FLORIDA*

Illustration: U.S. Navy Photo Department Washington D.C.

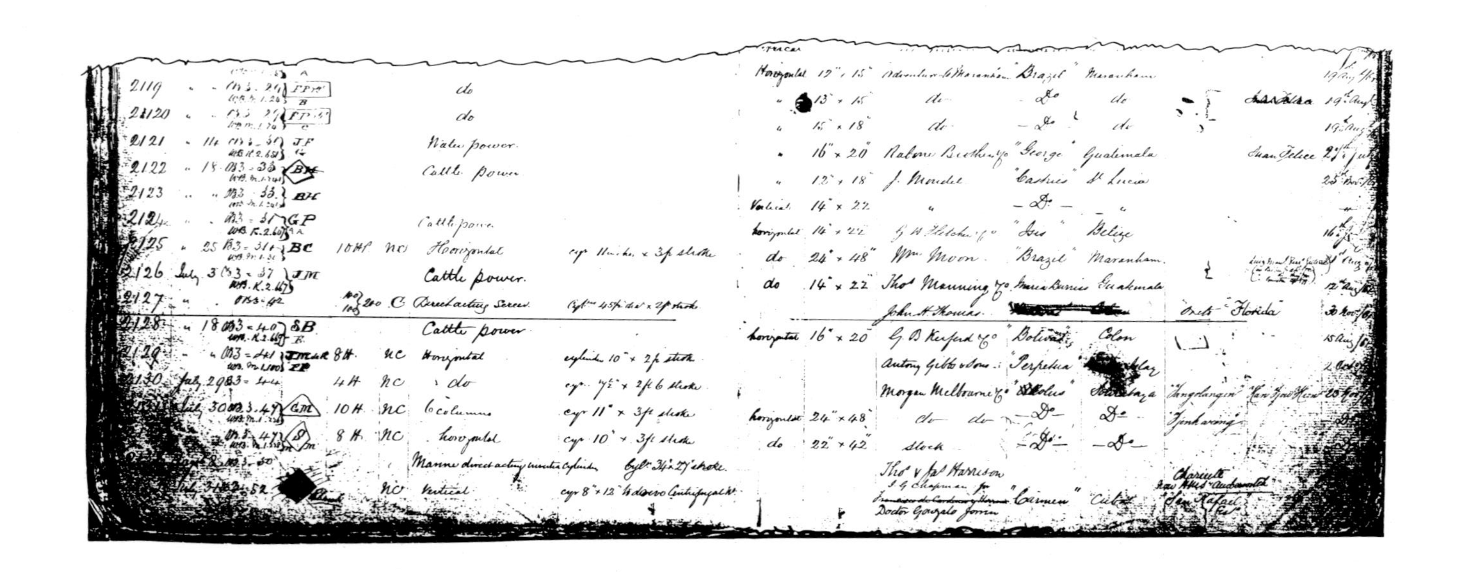

Engine Book of Fawcett & Preston (underlined entry) of the C.S.S. Florida.
Photo: Fawcett & Preston.

But just after the vessel left port, yellow fever struck Maffitt and most of his crew. Seriously ill as he was, Maffitt sailed the ship as far as Mobile, Alabama. Boldly the sick men raced their ship through the Union Blockade[1] Squadron in broad daylight and her great speed carried her past the Union ships.

A number of delays kept the Florida from sailing again until early 1863. This time, Maffitt went out at night. Again he eluded the blockaders, even though they had been alerted and reinforced to prevent the Florida's escape. For six months, the Florida cruised the Western Atlantic. Maffitt captured a total of twenty one ships, then to escape a pursuing Union squadron, he sailed for Brest, France, and there he had the Florida repaired and refitted. Early in 1864, she was on the high seas again, this time under Lt Charles M. Morris because Maffitt was sick again and had to be left behind.

The Florida made another wide sweep of the Atlantic and captured fifteen more Northern ships before she stopped at the port of Bahia, Brazil, to take on coal and other supplies.

The Union Sloop of War, Wachusetts was in Bahia Harbour at the time, Morris was not worried about the presence of the much stronger Northern ship because Bahia was a neutral port, but Commander Napoleon Collins of the Wachusetts was not a man to worry about International law. Two nights later he ran his ship into the side of the Confederate raider, quickly captured her, and took her back to Hampton Roads, Virginia.

The Union Government later apologised to Brazil for the brazen violation of her neutrality, but the Florida could not be returned. She had been sunk by "accident" in Hampton Roads, Virginia. Collins was tried by Court Martial and sentenced to be dismissed from the Union Navy. Gideon Welles dissaproved of the sentence and returned Collins to full duty. He refused to punish one of his officers for capturing a dangerous Southern raider, despite the violation of International Law.

[1] The Union Navy Blockaded Southern Ports to stop trade between the Confederacy and other nations. As the war progressed the Blockade tightened making it virtually impossible to sail in or out of a port.

C.S.S. ALABAMA

Photo: U.S. Navy Photo Department Washington D.C.

The Alabama, alias Enrica, built by Laird Brothers, left Liverpool on July 29th, 1862. Laird's described her as "the finest cruiser of her class in the world", such was the workmanship of Laird's. Four sternposts were fitted before the work was approved. The final cost of the Alabama was £47,046.

In temporary command was Captain Matthew J. Butcher, first officer of a Cunard liner. He was employed merely to take the ship to a rendezvous. Also on board was the English Confederate Officer John Low.[1] The majority of the crew had been recruited on the streets of Liverpool, "for a voyage to the Bahamas or possibly Havana".

After leaving Liverpool Bay, the Alabama sailed to Moelfre, Anglesey, where she spent two days preparing for sea. On the 31st July she entered the Irish Sea, where James Bulloch (the Confederate Agent) and the pilot

Statesmen. No. 144.

MR. JOHN LAIRD, M.P.

AMONG those who in doing their own business have contributed permanently to the material prosperity of the State Mr. Laird should take a high place, for he may be said to have invented and created a populous town and to have revolutionised the art of shipbuilding. Born at Greenock now sixty-eight years ago, he became engaged when scarcely yet a grown man in the business of an ironworks at what was then the forsaken little village of Birkenhead, owning for all its population but two hundred souls. The idea of constructing vessels of anything else than wood had then scarcely entered into any man's head; but young Laird took up the notion and, after building in 1829 nearly the first iron vessel launched, fought it through till iron has rivalled and in a great measure replaced its more ancient rival. He resolved moreover to set up Birkenhead by the side of Liverpool. His father had projected vast docks there, and it was given to the son to see them constructed and to be named one of the Commissioners to whom was handed over the water government not only of Birkenhead but of Liverpool as well. He watched over the town with the affection of a father. He successively built at his own cost and presented to his townsmen in 1862 a hospital and in 1871 a school of art, and it is natural therefore that for the last twelve years he should have represented the place he has made.

Mr. Laird, being rich, is a Conservative and a man of equable good temper and urbanity. He is also a keen sportsman, and so regular a follower of hounds that few figures are better known than his in the hunting-field. He is of a somewhat saddened and retiring disposition, but is personally popular with those who know him. In 1861 Mr. Laird retired with a fortune from the shipbuilding business which had made him so well-known, and which was thenceforth carried on by his sons. Almost coincidently with his retirement his firm contracted to build for the Government of the Confederate States, then in insurrection against the American Union, a vessel of war afterwards but too well-known as the *Alabama*. There is no doubt that they did this as a mere commercial transaction, and probably they did not suspect at the time that they would ever meet with aught but approbation for the undertaking. It soon became apparent however that the escape of this vessel was likely to bring about grave results, and in 1863 Mr. Laird was put upon his defence in the House of Commons. He then and there said, "I would "rather be handed down to posterity as the builder of a dozen *Alabamas* than as "the man (Mr. Bright) who applies himself deliberately to set class against class— "(loud cheers)—and to cry up the institutions of another country, which when they "come to be tested are of no value whatever, and which reduce liberty to an utter "absurdity. (Cheers.)" Not for the building of the *Alabama*, nor for her escape, but for the cheers with which British Legislators received these words has England now been hunted down to humiliation and the payment of three millions and a half of treasure—and the responsibility of the cheers does not lie on Mr. Laird. For all that his name will be coupled, not with statesmanship or policy, but with the national disgrace as long as memory remains of it; and although it be not literally true, it will in generations to come be said of him that he built the *Alabama* and the *Captain*, and was thus intimately connected with two gigantic national disasters.

Article from the Victorian Magazine Vanity Fair relating to John Laird M.P. synonomous with the Alabama incident.

No. 237. STATESMEN, No. 144.

"He built the 'Alabama' and the 'Captain.'"

were landed at the Giant's Causeway. The ship then sailed to Terceira in the Azores for the rendezvous with the supply ship Agrippina and the loading of guns, ammunition and provisions. Captain Raphael Semmes took charge of his new ship on the 13th August. She was commissioned into the Confederate Navy on the 24th with the stirring new anthem "Dixie" being played.

From August, 1862 till June 1864, the Alabama captured and burned fifty five Union merchantmen worth $4,500,000, and bonded[2] ten others to the value of $562,000. Another prize, Conrad, was commissioned C.S.S. Tuscaloosa, which also struck at Northern shipping. The Union Navy also felt the Alabama's sting when she sank the U.S.S. Hatteras off Galveston, Texas. On Sunday 19th, 1864 the Alabama met the U.S.S. Kearsage off Cherbourg, France, captained by John A. Winslow. The Alabama after almost two years at sea was in a bad condition, only being able to stay in port at Cherbourg for a short period owing to the neutrality regulations. Her copper botton was badly fouled which reduced her speed and her gunpowder was in poor condition. These facts were to tell in the ensuing battle.

The arrival of the Alabama and now the impending duel with the Kearsage, had caused a sensation in France and thousands lined the coast while others took to the sea in small boats to witness the spectacle. The Alabama fired the opening shots and throughout the action fired double that of the Kearsage, however, except for one shot from the Alabama that embedded itself in Kearsage's sternpost, but failed to explode, it was Kearsage's shots that found their mark. As the Alabama started to sink the steam yacht Deerhound (also built at Laird's) owned by John Lancaster from England appeared, to save a number of the crew who were swimming in the water, including Captain Semmes and a number of officers. The Deerhound landed the survivors at Southampton. On arrival in England Captain Semmes and his crew received a hero's welcome, and Semmes was inundated with gifts including a spectacular gold mounted sword presented by officers of the Royal Navy. Before his return to the Confederacy Captain Semmes recuperated at the house of the the Reverend F.W. Tremlett at Belsize Park London.

[1] John Low was brought up by relatives in Aberdeen and Liverpool, as his parents died shortly after his birth in 1836. He went to sea at the age of sixteen and in 1856, at the suggestion of his uncle Andrew Low, a wealthy Savannah businessman, he sailed to America. When war broke out, because of his nautical experience, he was ordered to England to help in the task of obtaining naval vessels for the Confederacy. During the cruise of the Alabama he took charge of the Conrad which was renamed C.S.S. Tuscaloosa. He set up in business in Liverpool after the war and is buried in Golborne Church Yard, Newton-le-Willows.

[2] When a vessel was bonded the Captain of the vessel signed an agreement that at the end of the war the value of the vessel would be paid to the Confederacy. (Of course this was only binding if the Confederate won the war.)

Raphael Semmes, Captain of the C.S.S. Alabama.
Illustration: U.S. Navy Photo Department Washington D.C.

Alec Henry Low, Grandson of John Low with pennant, picked up by a Frenchman after the Alabama/Kearsage duel, off Cherbourg. This was sent to John Low in Liverpool after the war. The pennant is of Union origin and is probably from the Kearsage. (Many of the Alabama's shots hit the Kearsage's rigging, thus dislodging the pennant.)

No. 290 Gunboat

213 3/4 x 31 3/4 x 18 = 1044 B.M. Keel laid July

Hull & Woodwork -

E. Oak, &c. 56837 cft [illegible] 10,4[illegible] 8 7

Sawing 893.10.11, Pine [illegible] 309.19.1 [illegible] 1588 18

Copper rods (Invoice 11½) — 1582 5

Compo [illegible] — 396 5 [illegible]

Nails, oakum, &c. — 287 [illegible]

Paint, &c. 96.4.9, Bolts [illegible] 181.7 [illegible]

5 Kingston Valves — [illegible]

Carpenters (Mould 271) 14052.6/6 [illegible]

Joiners (— do — 303) 1885 [illegible] 494 16 3

Labourers 4378 Painters 523 - 4901 [illegible]

Turning 16.17; planing 22.31, Scraping &c. [illegible] 34096 6 8

19697 11

Iron Beams, Straps, Bolts &c. 48 6 2 16 580 12 4

Casting (c 11/6) - 26 1 16 306 [illegible]

Galvanizing — [illegible]

Smiths 2879 589.15.11, Bolt 10 47/6 589 18 5

Machy 59 29.17, [illegible] [illegible]

Brass (Rudder & [illegible]) 489.15.3, [illegible] 30.13 [illegible]

Plumbing [illegible] 240.12.5 Cabinet [illegible] 406 [illegible] polish[illegible]

Carving, glazing & sundries — 98 [illegible]

Coppering bottom Sheets 8137.24. 10 846 5 2

Compo. Nails (& paper 5.19.7) 19 17

Carpenters 204 c 64

Masts & Spars - Timber (spare) 324 13 8

Paint Leather, nails &c. 16 17 3 341 [illegible]

Carps 277 83.21, Painting &c. [illegible] 435 12 11

A page of Laird's Ledger relating to the Alabama. Page shows material, labour costs.
The original is now in the Williamson Art Gallery Birkenhead.

C. S. Steamer Alabama
Decr. 6th, 1862

Lieut: Low will take charge of the Prize Steamer Ariel, with his prize crew, & follow my motions during the night. I shall run over to-night to the port of Nicolas Mole, in the N.W. end of St. Domingo, for the purpose of landing the passengers in the morning. As this port is only about fifty miles distant, & I do not wish to arrive much before daylight, it will only be necessary for me to make five or six miles per hour, so that you must carry very low steam. I will hoist a light at the peak, & I wish you to carry your mast head light during the night. I shall probably be ready to start at 7 o'clock, & as a signal that I am ready, I will hoist two lights at the peak — one under the other, which you will answer by hoisting one light at the peak. You must keep your men near you <u>all</u> night, & you will have to exercise the greatest vigilance to prevent them from getting drunk. I will send a couple of our engineers on board to assist you, & you must make the firemen, & crew of the prize perform their usual duty.

Yr &c
R. Semmes
Commander

Letter from Raphael Semmes to John Low ordering him to take charge of the Union vessel Ariel. Of particular note is Semmes instruction to Low to prevent the prize crew from getting drunk.
Photocopy: Alec Low, Tasmania.

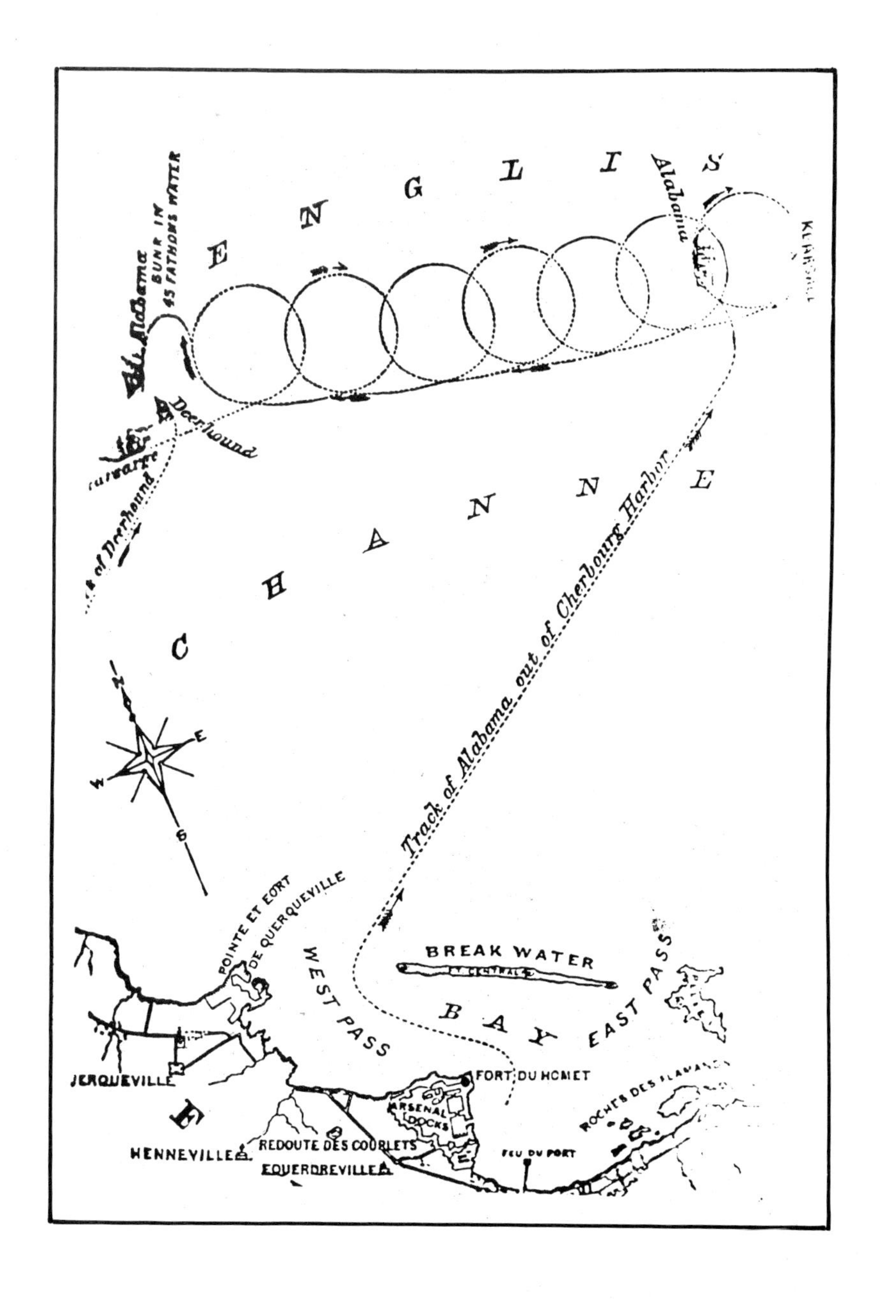

This chart diagrams the battle between Alabama and Kearsage.
Illustration: U.S. Navy Photo Department Washington D.C.

Duel off Cherbourg between the Alabama and the Kearsage: Sinking of the Alabama. Illustration: U.S. Navy Photo Department Washington D.C.

Such was the fame of the Alabama that songs were composed about her. Shown above the first page of one of the many song sheets produced. Illustration: U.S. Navy Photo Department Washington D.C.

C.S.S. SHENANDOAH

The C.S.S. Shenandoah originally Sea King was built on the River Clyde and purchased by the Government of the Confederacy in 1864 for use as an armed-cruiser. She was an iron framed, teakplanked, fullrigged vessel with auxiliary steam power. The ship was designed to transport troops to the Far East.

On 8th October, she sailed from London ostensibly for Bombay, India, on a trading voyage. At Funchal, Madeira, she kept a rendezvous with the steamer, Laurel, which carried officers and the nucleus of a crew for Sea King, together with guns, ammunition, and stores. The Commanding Officer, Lt J.I. Waddell, supervised her conversion to a ship-of-war. Waddell was barely able however to bring his crew to half strength. The new cruiser was commissioned on 19th October and her name changed to Shenandoah. On route to the Cape of Good Hope she picked up six prizes, five of these were put to the torch or scuttled, the other was bonded and employed for transport of prisoners to Bahia, Brazil.[1] Still shorthanded, despite recent additions, Shenandoah arrived at Melbourne, Australia, on 25th January, 1865 where she made up her complement and filled her storerooms. Shenandoah had only taken one prize in the Indian Ocean, but hunting became more profitable as she approached the whaling grounds. Waddell burned four whalers in the Carolines and another off the Kuriles. A three week cruise in the ice and fog off the Sea of Okhotsk failed to yield a single prize, because Union ships had been warned. Waddell steered north, past the Aleutian Islands into the Barents Sea and the Arctic Ocean. On 23rd June, he learned from a prize of Lee's surrender and the flight from Richmond of the Confederate Government ten weeks previously. Nevertheless, he elected to continue hostilities, and captured twenty one more prizes, the last eleven being

The Confederate cruiser Shenandoah in the River Mersey. Illustration: London Illus. News.

taken in the space of seven hours in the waters just below the Arctic Circle.

Waddell then ran south to intercept commerce bound from the West Coast to the Far East and Latin America, and on the 2nd August received news of the war's end some four months earlier. Immediately Shenandoah underwent physical alteration. Her armaments were dismantled and put below, and her hull painted to resemble a merchant vessel. Waddell decided to sail her to England and chose Liverpool as the port of surrender. He arrived on 6th November, 1865 where the pilot ordered that she should be anchored near H.M.S. Donegal. All on board were confined to the vessel by order of the port authorities. On 10th November, the crew were unconditionally released, the surrender and other negotiations being concluded with Captain Paynter of H.M.S. Donegal. Shenandoah had remained at sea for twelve months and seventeen days, had traversed 58,000 miles and captured thirty eight prizes, mostly whalers, two-thirds of them after the close of hostilities.

The Shenandoah was turned over to the United States by the British authorities. She was later sold and served various owners eventually being lost in the Indian Ocean under the flag of the Sultan of Zanzibar.

[1] Bahia being the nearest convient port where the prisoners could be landed.

C.S.S. TALLAHASSEE

The C.S.S. Tallahassee, formerly the blockade-runner Atalanta was built at Millwall on the Thames and had passed through the Union Navy blockade on several occasions at Wilmington, North Carolina. She was commissioned into the Confederate Navy in early 1864, under the command of Commodore J.T. Wood.

On 6th August, 1864, the Tallahassee was taken through the blockade and during a nineteen day period sailing off the east coast of America and Canada twenty six vessels were destroyed. She returned to Wilmington on the 26th August owing to shortage of coal.

Renamed the Olustee under a new commander Lt W.H. Ward, she again sailed through the blockade suffering some damage from the Union ships. Off the coast of Delaware she captured and sank six merchant vessels, returning to Wilmington for more coal. On November 6th, she avoided attempts by the Sassacus and four other Union men-of-war to capture her and again reached Wilmington on 7th November.

After these successful voyages, the ship was renamed Chameleon and the battery was removed. Captained by Lt J. Wilkinson, she sailed through the blockade on the 24th December, having no trouble with the Union navy as they were more preocupied with the bombardment of nearby Fort Fisher. The Chameleon sailed to Bermuda to obtain supplies for the Confederate army. On her return to the Southern States she attempted to enter two different ports without success. The decision was made to sail her to Liverpool and hand her over to the Confederate agent, James Bulloch.

The Chameleon arrived in Liverpool on the 9th April, 1865 and was seized and then sold by the British authorities. Hearing of the seizure the United States government issued a suit for her possession and she was handed over to the U.S. consul on 26th April, 1866.

The C.S.S. Tallahassee. Illustration: London Illus. News.

THE ALABAMA CLAIM

After the American Civil War, the United States Government demanded that damages should be paid by the British Authorities for the destruction caused by the Confederate cruisers. The vessels, Alabama, Florida, and the Shenandoah alone had accounted for one half of the Union vessels captured during hostilities by the Southern high seas raiders. Since the Alabama had caused the most damage the American demand was known as the "Alabama Claim".

The United States Government's claim was based on international law that a neutral nation should not allow its sea ports to be used to support the navy of a country at war. The American authorities said that Great Britain had permitted the Confederate Government to purchase the three raiders in England and that these vessels had used British ports around the globe as their bases.

After long discussions between the two Governments, it was agreed to submit the matter to an International Arbitration Commission. The Commission approved the American claim in 1873 and Great Britain was forced to pay £3,000,000 in compensation.

ACKNOWLEDGMENTS

I would like to thank the following people and organizations for their assistance in helping me compile this booklet.

Darroch D.	Cammell Laird.
Campbell E.D.C.	Museum of the Confederacy, Richmond, Virginia.
Crippen Miss K.M.	Liverpool.
Fawcett & Preston	Bromborough, Merseyside.
Fonvielle C.	Blockade-Runners Museum, Carolina Beach, North Carolina.
Fox K.	Cammell Laird, Birkenhead.
Hensley P.B.	Mariners Museum, Newport News, Virginia.
Holcombe R.	Confederate Naval Museum, Columbus, Georgia.
Lane M.B.	Ships of the Sea Museum, Savannah, Georgia.
Laird G.	Newcastle Upon Tyne.
Low A.	London.
McLoone H.	Huntington Library, San Marino, California.
Moore L.	London Illustrated News.
Mason H.	Birkenhead.
Peery Dr. C.	Charleston, South Carolina.
Roberts J.K.	Birkenhead.
Sweetingham J.	Tasmania.
Thornton C.	Curator, Williamson Art Gallery & Museum, Birkenhead.
Tilley J.A.	Mariners Museum, Newport News, Virginia.
William Brown Street Library	Liverpool.
Willingham R.M.	University of Georgia Libraries.

SELECTED BIBLIOGRAPHY

Bacon J.	Classic Ships C.S.S. Alabama, Model Shipwright No.22 1977.
Boykin E.	Ghost Ship of the Confederacy.
County Borough of Birkenhead	Birkenhead 1877-1974.
Cook A.	Alabama Claims.
Delaney N.C.	John McIntosh Kell of the Raider Alabama.
Hill J.D.	Sea Dogs of the Sixties.
Hoole W.S.	Four Years in the Confederate Navy.
Hoole W.S.	Logs of the C.S.S. Alabama & C.S.S. Tuscaloosa.
Horan J.D.	C.S.S. Shenandoah.
John E.	Atlantic Impact 1861.
Merlie F.J.	Great Britain & The Confederate Navy 1861-1865.
Robinson W.H.	The Confederate Privateers.
Sharf J.T.	History of the Confederate States Navy 1861-1865.
Summersell C.	The Journal of George Townley Fullam.
U.S. Navy History Division	Civil War Naval Chronology Volumes 1 to 6.
Vandiver F.E.	Confederate Blockade Runners through Bermuda.
Washington Government Print Office 1895	Official Records of the Confederate & Union Navies 1861-1862.
White H.	"Fossets" The Story of Fawcett & Preston.

UNITED STATES VESSELS DESTROYED BY CONFEDERATE CRUISERS

VESSELS DESTROYED BY THE ALABAMA

When destroyed	*Name of Vessel*	*Character*	*Property destroyed*	*Value*
Sept. 9, 1862	**Alert**	*Ship*	Vessel & outfits	$**52,000**
Sept. 13, 1862	**Altamaha**	*Brig*	Brig, outfits	**6,000**
Nov. 6, 1863	**Amanda**	*Bark*	Vessel & freight	**104,442**
June 2, 1863	**Amazonian**	*Bark*	Bark & charter	**97,665**
July 2, 1863	**Anna F. Schmidt**	*Ship*	Dif. val & ins.	**350,000**
Dec. 7, 1862	**Ariel**	*Steamer*	Bonded U.S. Treasury Notes	**261,000**
Oct. 29, 1862	**Baron de Castine**	*Brig*	Bonded	**6,000**
Sept. 14, 1862	**Benj. Tucker**	*Ship*	Vessel, outfit etc.	**70,200**
March 1, 1863	**Bethia Thayer**	*Ship*	Bonded	**40,000**
Oct. 3, 1862	**Brilliant**	*Ship*	Bonded	**164,000**
March 25, 1863	**Charles Hill**	*Ship*	Bonded	**28,450**
Jan. 27, 1863	**Chastelaine**	*Brig*	Vessel & Cargo	**10,000**
Nov. 21, 1862	**Clara L. Sparks**	*Schooner*	"	———
June 19, 1863	**Conrad**	*Bark*	"	**69,000**
Nov. 11, 1863	**Contest**	*Ship*	"	**122,815**
Sept. 16, 1862	**Courser**	*Schooner*	"	**7,000**
Oct. 26, 1862	**Crenshaw**	*"*	"	**33,869**
April 26, 1863	**Dorcas Prince**	*Ship*	"	**44,108**
Oct. 7, 1862	**Dunkirk**	*Brig*	"	**25,000**
Sept. 18, 1862	**Elisha Dunbar**	*Bark*	"	**27,000**
Oct. 3, 1862	**Emily Farnum**	*Ship*	Released	———
Jan. 14, 1864	**Emma Jane**	*Ship*	Vessel & charter	**40,000**
July 6, 1863	**Express**	*Ship*	Vessel & freight	**121,300**
Feb. 21, 1863	**Golden Eagle**	*Ship*	"	**61,000**
Jan. 26, 1863	**Golden Rule**	*Bark*	"	**112,000**
Nov. 18, 1863	**Harriet Spalding**	*Bark*	———	———
Jan. 11, 1863	**Hatteras**	*Gunboat*	———	**160,000**
Dec. 26, 1863	**Highlander**	*Ship*	Vessel & freight	**75,965**
May 29, 1863	**Jabez Snow**	*Ship*	"	**72,881**
March 2, 1863	**John A. Parks**	*Ship*	"	**70,000**
May 25, 1863	**Justina**	*Bark*	———	**7,000**

April 15, 1863	**Kate Cory**	*Brig*	Vessel etc.	**28,268**
March 26, 1863	**Kingfisher**	*Schooner*	Vessel etc.	**24,000**
Oct. 23, 1862	**Lafayette (1)**	*Ship*	"	**110,337**
April 15, 1863	**Lafayette (2)**	*Bark*	"	**36,025**
Oct. 15, 1862	**Lamplighter**	*Bark*	"	**117,600**
Oct. 28, 1862	**Lauretta**	*Bark*	"	**32,800**
Nov. 2, 1862	**Levi Starbuck**	*Ship*	"	**203,962**
April 4, 1863	**Louisa Hatch**	*Ship*	"	**82,250**
Oct. 11, 1862	**Manchester**	______	"	**164,000**
Aug. 9, 1863	**Martha Wenzell**	*Bark*	Released	______
Dec. 24, 1863	**Martaban**	*Ship*	Vessel etc.	**97,628**
March 23, 1863	**Morning Star**	*Ship*	Bonded	**61,750**
Dec. 5, 1862	**Nina**	*Ship*	Bonded	______
March 25, 1863	**Nora**	*Ship*	Vessel etc.	**80,000**
April 24, 1862	**Nye**	*Bark*	"	**31,127**
Sept. 8, 1862	**Ocean Rover**	*Bark*	"	**98,820**
Sept. 5, 1862	**Ocmulgee**	*Ship*	"	**131,712**
Feb. 21, 1863	**Olive Jane**	*Bark*	Merchandise	**43,208**
Feb. 3, 1863	**Palmetto**	*Schooner*	"	**18,434**
Nov. 30, 1862	**Parker Cook**	*Bark*	Vessel etc.	**25,399**
March 15, 1863	**Punjab**	*Ship*	Bonded	**52,000**
April 23, 1864	**Rockingham**	*Ship*	Vessel etc.	**105,000**
Aug. 5, 1863	**Sea Bride**	*Bark*	"	**100,000**
May 3, 1863	**Sea Lark**	*Ship*	"	**550,000**
May 25, 1863	**S. Gildersleeve**	*Ship*	"	**62,783**
Dec. 26, 1863	**Sonora**	*Ship*	"	**46,545**
Sept. 7, 1862	**Starlight**	*Schooner*	"	**4,000**
June 5, 1863	**Talisman**	*Ship*	"	**139,135**
Nov. 8, 1862	**Thomas B. Wales**	*Ship*	"	**245,625**
Oct. 9, 1862	**Tonawanda**	*Ship*	Bonded	**80,000**
April 27, 1864	**Tycoon**	*Bark*	Vessel etc.	**88,559**
Dec. 5, 1862	**Union**	*Schooner*	Bonded	**1,500**
May 3, 1863	**Union Jack**	*Bark*	Vessel etc.	**77,000**
Sept. 17, 1862	**Virginia**	*Ship*	"	**30,074**
Feb. 27, 1863	**Washington**	*Ship*	Bonded	**50,000**
Oct. 7, 1862	**Wave Crest**	*Bark*	Vessel etc.	**44,000**
Sept. 9, 1862	**Weather Gage**	*Schooner*	"	**10,000**
Nov. 10, 1863	**Winged Racer**	*Ship*	"	**150,000**

VESSELS DESTROYED BY THE FLORIDA

When destroyed	***Name of Vessel***	***Character***	***Property destroyed***	***Value***
March 13, 1863	**Aldebaran**	*Schooner*	Vessel etc.	**$22,998**
Aug. 20, 1863	**Anglo Saxon**	*Ship*	"	______
Jan. 12, 1863	**Arabella**	*Brig*	"	______
______	**B.F. Hoxie**	*Ship*	"	**70,000**
May 6, 1863	**Clarence**	*Brig*	______	______

April 17, 1863	**Commonwealth**	*Ship*	Vessel, etc.	**352,000**
Jan. 22, 1863	**Corris Ann**	*Brig*	Cargo, etc.	—
May 13, 1863	**Crown Point**	*Ship*	Personal prop. etc.	—
—	**David Lapsley**	*Bark*	—	—
July 10, 1864	**Electric Spark**	*Steamer*	Cargo, etc.	**166,000**
Jan. 19, 1863	**Estelle**	*Brig*	Vessel etc.	**12,000**
Aug. 6, 1863	**Francis B. Cutting**	*Ship*	—	—
May 18, 1864	**Geo. Latimer**	*Schooner*	Bonded	—
July 10, 1863	**Gen. Berry**	*Bark*	—	—
July 8, 1864	**Golconda**	*Bark*	Vessel etc.	—
—	**Greenland**	*Bark*	Personal prop. etc.	—
July 1, 1864	**Harriet Stevens**	*Bark*	Vessel etc.	**10,500**
April 23, 1863	**Henrietta**	*Bark*	"	**57,049**
Feb. 12, 1863	**Jacob Bell**	*Ship*	"	**1,500,000**
June 17, 1863	**Kate Dye**	*Ship*	—	—
March 9, 1863	**Lapwing**	*Bark*	Vessel & cargo	**77,000**
July 9, 1863	**Margaret W. Davis**	*Schooner*	—	—
March 13, 1863	**M.J. Colcord**	*Bark*	Vessel & cargo	—
Sept. 26, 1864	**Mondamin**	*Bark*	"	—
April 24, 1864	**Oneida**	*Ship*	"	**760,000**
June, 1863	**Red Gauntlet**	*Ship*	Vessel & cargo	—
July 8, 1863	**Rienzi**	*Schooner*	"	—
June 6, 1863	**Southern Cross**	*Ship*	"	—
Aug. 22, 1863	**Southern Rights**	*Ship*	Bonded	—
March 6, 1863	**Star of Peace**	*Ship*	Vessel etc.	—
July 7, 1863	**Sunrise**	*Ship*	Bonded	**60,000**
June 26, 1863	**Varnum H. Hill**	*Schooner*	Bonded	**70,000**
July 8, 1863	**Wm. B. Nash**	*Brig*	Vessel & cargo	—
Jan. 22, 1863	**Windward**	*Brig*	"	—
June 17, 1864	**Wm. C. Clark**	*Brig*	—	—
June 10, 1864	**Zelinda**	*Bark*	—	—

VESSELS DESTROYED BY THE SHENANDOAH

When destroyed	***Name of Vessel***	***Character***	***Property destroyed***	***Value***
May 27, 1865	**Abigail**	*Bark*	Vessel etc.	**$74,659**
—	**Adelaide**	*Bark*	Bonded	**24,000**
Dec. 4, 1864	**Alina**	*Bark*	Vessel etc.	**95,000**
Oct. 30, 1864	**Brunswick**	*Ship*	"	**16,272**
June 26, 1865	**Catherine**	*Bark*	"	**26,174**
Nov. 5, 1865	**Charter Oak**	*Schooner*	"	**15,000**

June 28, 1865	**Congress**	*Schooner*	"	**90,827**
June 28, 1865	**Covington**	*Bark*	"	**43,764**
Dec. 29, 1864	**Delphine**	*Bark*	"	**76,000**
Nov. 8, 1864	**D. Godfrey**	*Bark*	"	**36,000**
Dec. 4, 1864	**Edward**	*Bark*	"	**20,000**
April 1, 1865	**Edward Casey**	*Ship*	"	**109,582**
June 21, 1865	**Euphrates**	*Ship*	"	**168,688**
June 28, 1865	**Favorite**	*Bark*	"	**130,000**
June 26, 1865	**Gen. Pike**	*Bark*	Ransomed	———
June 26, 1865	**Gipsey**	*Bark*	Vessel etc.	**80,000**
April 1, 1865	**Harvest**	*Bark*	"	**34,759**
April 1, 1865	**Hector**	*Ship*	"	**75,000**
June 28, 1865	**Fillmore**	*Ship*	"	**71,451**
June 28, 1865	**Isaac Howard**	*Ship*	Vessel etc.	**115,000**
June 26, 1865	**Isabella**	*Bark*	"	**87,765**
June 28, 1865	**James Maury**	*Bark*	Ransomed	———
June 24, 1865	**Jireh Swift**	*Bark*	Vessel etc.	**61,960**
Nov. 12, 1864	**Kate Prince**	*Ship*	Bonded	———
Nov. 13, 1864	**Lizzie M. Stacey**	*Schooner*	Vessel etc.	**30,000**
June 28, 1865	**Martha**	*Bark*	"	**65,000**
June 28, 1865	**Nassau**	*Ship*	"	**89,424**
June 28, 1865	**Nile**	*Bark*	Bonded	**25,500**
June 26, 1865	**Nimrod**	*Bark*	Vessel etc.	**29,260**
April 1, 1865	**Pearl**	*Bark*	"	**10,000**
June 24, 1865	**Sophia Thornton**	*Ship*	"	**70,000**
Nov. 10, 1865	**Susan**	*Bark*	"	**5,436**
June 25, 1865	**Susan & Abigail**	*Brig*	"	**225,848**
June 28, 1865	**Waverly**	*Bark*	"	**84,655**
June 22, 1865	**Wm Thompson**	*Ship*	"	**105,093**
June 26, 1865	**Wm C. Nye**	*Bark*	"	**62,087**

VESSELS DESTROYED BY THE TALLAHASSEE

When destroyed	*Name of Vessel*	*Character*	*Property destroyed*	*Value*
Aug. 12, 1864	**Adriatic**	*Ship*	Vessel etc.	$ ———
Aug. 11, 1864	**A. Richards**	*Brig*	———	———
———	**Atlantic**	*Schooner*	———	———
Aug. 11, 1864	**Bay State**	*Bark*	———	———
Aug. 10, 1864	**Billow**	*Brig*	———	———
Aug. 11, 1864	**Carrie Estelle**	*Brig*	———	———
———	**Castine**	*Ship*	———	———
Aug. 11, 1864	**Coral Heath**	*Brig*	———	———
Aug. 10, 1864	**Etta Caroline**	*Steamer*	———	———
Aug. 15, 1864	**Floral Wreath**	*Schooner*	Vessel etc.	———
———	**Glenavon**	*Bark*	"	———
Aug. 12, 1864	**Goodspeed**	*Schooner*	———	———

Aug. 12, 1864	**Howard**	*Bark*	———	———
Aug. 11, 1864	**James Funk**	*Pilot-boat*	———	**24,000**
Aug. 14, 1864	**James Littlefield**	*Ship*	———	———
Aug. 14, 1864	**J.H. Howen**	*Schooner*	———	———
Aug. 17, 1864	**Josiah Achorne**	*Schooner*	———	**8,000**
Aug. 13, 1864	**Lamont Dupont**	*Schooner*	———	———
Aug. 15, 1864	**Magnolia**	*Schooner*	———	———
Aug. 15, 1864	**Mercy A. Howes**	*Schooner*	———	———
Aug. 17, 1864	**North America**	*Schooner*	Vessel etc.	———
———	**P.C. Alexander**	*Bark*	———	———
Aug. 16, 1864	**Pearl**	*Schooner*	———	———
Aug. 23, 1864	**Restless**	*Schooner*	———	———
Aug. 20, 1864	**Rowan**	*Schooner*	———	———
Aug. 11, 1864	**Sarah A. Boyce**	*Schooner*	———	———
———	**Sarah Louisa**	*Schooner*	———	———
Aug. 12, 1864	**Spokane**	*Schooner*	———	———
Aug. 11, 1864	**William Bell**	*Pilot-boat*	———	**24,000**

VESSELS DESTROYED BY THE OLUSTEE (FORMERLY TALLSHASSEE)

When destroyed	*Name of Vessel*	*Character*	*Property destroyed*	*Value*
Nov. 3, 1864	**A.J. Bird**	*Schooner*	Vessel etc.	$**24,869**
Nov. 3, 1864	**Arcole**	*Ship*	Cargo	**18,000**
Nov. 3, 1864	**E.F. Lewis**	*Schooner*	Vessel etc.	———
Nov. 1, 1864	**Empress Theresa**	*Bark*	"	**30,000**
Nov. 3, 1864	**T.D. Wagner**	*Brig*	"	———
Nov. 3, 1864	**Vapor**	*Schooner*	Cargo	———